D0438942

MINDFUL ME

Mindfulness and Meditation for Kids

MINDFUL ME

Mindfulness and Meditation for Kids

Whitney Stewart

pictures by
Stacy Peterson

Albert Whitman & Company
Chicago, Illinois

Also by Whitney Stewart
Mindful Me Activity Book
Meditation Is an Open Sky: Mindfulness for Kids
A Catfish Tale

Library of Congress Cataloging-in-Publication Data

Names: Stewart, Whitney, author.
Title: Mindful me : mindfulness and meditation for kids / Whitney Stewart.
Description: Chicago, Illinois : Albert Whitman and Company, [2018]
Identifiers: LCCN 2017038022 | ISBN 9780807551448 (hardcover)
Subjects: LCSH: Meditation for children—Juvenile literature. |
Mindfulness (Psychology)—Juvenile literature. | Awareness—Juvenile literature.
Classification: LCC BF723.M37 S743 2018 | DDC 158.1/2083—dc23
LC record available at https://lccn.loc.gov/2017038022

Mindfulness practice is a resource. It is not a substitute for medical treatment.
If you have any concerns, please consult your health care provider
before you start a mindfulness practice.

Printed in the United States of America
10 9 8 7 6 5 4 3 2 1 BP 22 21 20 19 18

Design by Jordan Kost and Ellen Kokontis

For more information about Albert Whitman & Company,
visit our website at www.albertwhitman.com.

To Penelope and Lise,
who helped and inspired

Contents

Becoming a MINDFUL ME

Easy and Hard

You probably already know that some days life feels easy and fun, and other days everything goes wrong. You might have an argument with a friend or sibling and not know how to settle it or handle your angry feelings. Or, maybe school is hard and homework piles up. You could feel overwhelmed by everything you have to do, but be afraid to ask for help.

Then there are times when you're so excited about an upcoming event that you can't stop your brain from thinking about it. Maybe you're about to play in a soccer match or perform your first piano recital. A little stress can be good for you, because it pushes you to prepare. But what happens when you can't turn off your worries? Do you end up with a stomachache or have trouble falling asleep?

And what about loneliness? Sometimes you might feel like you don't fit into the popular crowd no matter what you do. Have you ever felt like that? Maybe other kids don't understand your passion for collecting spiders or doing crossword puzzles. That doesn't mean these aren't cool hobbies—they are!—but you could find yourself doing them alone.

You might think you're the only one with these challenges, but the truth is, everyone has hard times. Really, everyone! You can't control these situations. But you *can* control how you deal with them. Do you get angry and yell when things don't go your way? Do you cry or hide? Do you act out so people will pay attention to you? Or do you pretend nothing's wrong and hide your sad feelings? We all find ways to cope, but sometimes we make the situation worse when our methods are not skillful.

That's where MINDFUL ME PRACTICE comes in. Think of it as learning techniques for handling your life with wisdom. Instead of complaining and stressing about your bad luck or bullies or homework, you could learn to face whatever is happening and let it teach you something. Use the situation to make you stronger, or to make changes.

With MINDFUL ME PRACTICE, you can become a mountain, solid in any storm.

What Is MINDFUL ME PRACTICE?

When you practice MINDFUL ME exercises, you are practicing *mindfulness*. Mindfulness means paying attention, on purpose, to what's happening around you and inside you right now, without judging things as good or bad. You become curious about your experiences in a friendly way. You notice the details of whatever is happening through **present-moment awareness.**

Awareness is noticing and knowing. Here's an example of present-moment awareness. Imagine you are looking at a bee sitting on a flower. You are simply watching the bee with full attention. You notice the bee's shape and colors. You hear the bee's soft buzz. You notice the bee's antennae moving. You notice how the flower bends a little when the bee is sitting on it. All of your attention is on the bee.

When your mind loses present-moment awareness, it starts narrating like this: "Oh, bees are scary. I wonder if the bee will sting me. I don't like bees because they hurt when they sting. Are there more bees? What if I get stung? Do I have to go to the doctor?" These are thoughts you are having *about* bees. They are not observations *of* the bee.

If you are allergic to bees, this is a useful line of thinking that tells you to move away from the bee. But many of us are not allergic, and yet we get distracted and upset by imagining that the bee is a threat to us.

When that happens, you're back in your head, thinking and worrying. And the more thinking and worrying you do, the more stress you could feel.

But if you are simply practicing present-moment awareness of mindfulness, you will notice you were distracted and shift your attention back to the bee on the flower.

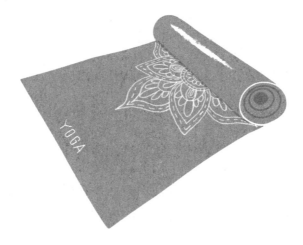

How Can Present-Moment Awareness Help?

So you've seen the bee on the flower. Maybe you got distracted but redirected your attention to studying and mindfully observing the bee. Perhaps you are feeling more relaxed and calmer. But why? What about this present-moment awareness of mindfulness can help you?

Let's look at present-moment awareness of your inner experiences. You might notice that when you have a busy mind full of anxious thoughts, you feel stress. If you obsess about something and avoid doing anything about it, the situation often grows worse.

However, when you use your present-moment awareness to notice and identify what's going on inside you—your thoughts, emotions, and physical sensations—you can begin to respond to your stress with strategies that calm you down and improve your health and happiness.

In other words, you need to become aware of a problem before you can find ways to deal with it.

Why Be Mindful?

Still not convinced mindfulness will help? Let's review the benefits of mindfulness that scientists and doctors have discovered:

Increased Awareness

Mindfulness practice helps you to develop your present-moment awareness of both your outer experiences—like the bee on the flower—and your inner experiences. Your thoughts, emotions, and physical sensations are all part of your inner experiences. This increased awareness can help you because it allows you to develop strategies for your health and wellness. When you have a toolbox of strategies, you often feel a greater sense of well-being and experience less pain and distress.

Focus and Attention

Mindfulness won't take away those homework problems we talked about, but it could help you pay attention and focus, so you study better and improve your grades.

Handling Emotions

Mindfulness won't make other kids magically love your spider collection, but it could help you manage disappointment when you feel left out or unhappy. That's because regular mindfulness practice often results in changes in your brain that help you handle uncomfortable feelings more easily.

Less Stress and Anxiety

Mindfulness practice will not stop your friends or siblings from bugging you. It will not take away all conflicts. But it might reduce your feelings of anger or stress when you're under pressure. Why? Because those brain changes we discussed also help you respond to conflicts with less fear, anger, and anxiety.

Understanding Helpful or Unhelpful Stress

In MINDFUL ME PRACTICE, you learn the difference between positive stress (*eustress*) and negative stress or worry. How can stress be good for you? Sometimes when you face a challenge, like preparing for a test or practicing for a performance, *eustress* motivates you. It makes you sharp and gives you energy to go out there and perform well. If stress keeps you from sleeping, gives you a headache or stomachache, or causes you to harm yourself, that's when you should ask for help. If you pay attention, you will know when stress is helping you or hurting you.

Increased Feelings of Kindness

Mindfulness also helps you understand that other people have thoughts and emotions much like yours. When you become aware of this, you can develop your understanding and compassion for other people. And when people are kind to each other, they feel closer and build a community.

What Is in MINDFUL ME PRACTICE?

MINDFUL ME PRACTICE includes developing a routine of awareness exercises, relaxation techniques, and meditation. The point of using this book is to find the exercises that best help you focus, notice what's going on inside and out, increase your present-moment awareness, and accept situations so you can deal with them in a positive way.

Mindfulness Takes Practice

You might be ready now to start MINDFUL ME PRACTICE. One point to know before you do is that nobody masters mindfulness on one try. (Too bad! Wouldn't it be great to snap your fingers and master your mind?) Mindfulness takes practice. Baby steps before giant leaps. That's important to remember, so let's highlight it:

Mindfulness takes practice.

If you forget to be mindful one day, don't worry. We all do that. No need to scold yourself. Instead, say, "Oops!" and start again.

The **past** is *over*. You can only make changes in the **present moment**. Right NOW! Each moment is another chance to be a MINDFUL ME.

Become a MINDFUL ME

So, let's recap. We all have challenges and need ways to deal with those challenges and respond positively to life. MINDFUL ME PRACTICE includes techniques that may improve your awareness and well-being. And finally, this book guides you through many different mindfulness exercises so you can learn what helps you most.

Here's the Takeaway

MINDFUL ME pays attention to the inside and also to the outside. MINDFUL ME notices the thoughts, feelings, and body sensations you are having right now and understands how they affect you. MINDFUL ME takes responsibility for your actions and attitudes, and trusts your inner goodness. MINDFUL ME cares for you and for the people (and animals) around you. MINDFUL ME uses helpful techniques to respond to life with wisdom and awareness.

Make a commitment to yourself.

Become a MINDFUL ME.

Chapter 1
MINDFUL ME Toolbox

What's Inside?

This book is a toolbox of mindfulness practices: exercises, activities, journal prompts, and meditation guides. See which ones help you the most. You might not like all of them. That's okay. Everyone is different. There are no hard rules in mindfulness—only helpful pointers.

Writing and drawing about your thoughts and feelings could help you understand them. You might see a problem in a new way. You can keep everything you write and draw in your MINDFUL ME Activity Book, or use your own MINDFUL ME binder or notebook. Check back any time and see how you have grown and changed.

MINDFUL ME Meditation

What Is Meditation?

Meditation is an important part of MINDFUL ME PRACTICE. In meditation, you stay alert and rest your mind in its calm, relaxed, and natural state.

What *is* the mind's natural state? That's hard to explain, but you experience it as an awareness or knowing that you are not the *center* of the universe but an important part of it. You're not an isolated dot in the middle, but one piece of a giant puzzle. And so is everyone else. That helps you see you are not alone. What you do affects your entire community and the whole planet.

Meditation also shows you that life is a flow, and everything is always changing. The Earth rotates, and the sun rises and sets. Seeds grow into plants that live out their life span. You were once a baby, and soon you'll be an adult. When you accept this ever-changing flow instead of struggling with it, you might find more peace in your heart. You can relax a little when things aren't going your way because you know they will change.

When you settle your mind, body, and breath in meditation, you may experience your natural state.

And if you don't, just wait and try again. Remember the guidelines—mindfulness and meditation take practice.

How to Sit in Meditation

To practice meditation, sit in a chair or cross-legged on a mat or blanket. Place an extra pillow under your bottom to help your posture. Sit up straight—as if you were a tall mountain—but not stiff. Relax your shoulders and jaw. Rest your hands on your thighs or in your lap. Keep your eyes slightly open and stare at a spot on the floor in front of you. If that distracts you, you can close your eyes until you're settled and then open them a little.

The benefits of keeping your eyes open are that you will be less likely to fall asleep and more likely to focus your mind. Some of the relaxation exercises in this book, however, do suggest you close your eyes. Find out what works best for you.

Begin each meditation with three MINDFUL ME BREATHS, described below. Relax all your muscles, and let your body sink into your seat. Let yourself be alert but relaxed.

You can start by taking three MINDFUL ME BREATHS.

Examine these images of meditation posture.
Choose one that allows you to be relaxed
with a straight spine, and alert.

Seiza

Quarter Lotus

Full Lotus

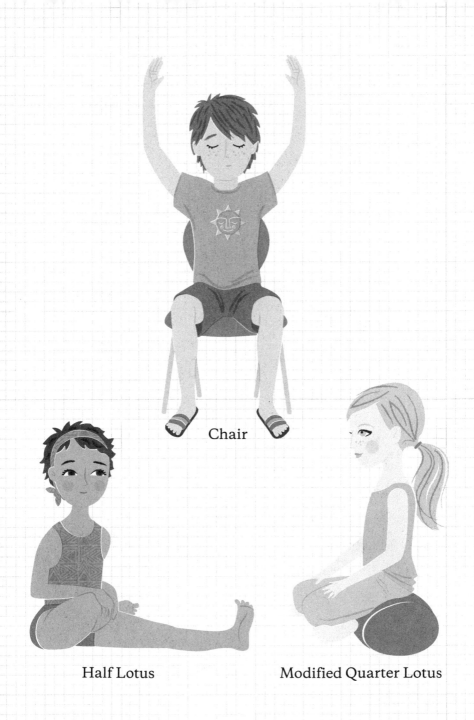

Chair

Half Lotus

Modified Quarter Lotus

Three MINDFUL ME BREATHS

As you begin, notice your breathing. Take three soft, slow breaths, and feel them in your body.

Breathe in, and feel air coming into your nose.

Breathe out, and count one.

Breathe in, and notice air filling your lungs.

Breathe out, and count two.

Breathe in, and see the air expanding your belly.

Breathe out, and count three.

Repeat for two more rounds of breathing into your nose, lungs, and belly.

Take three MINDFUL ME BREATHS any time you want to settle down and focus your attention. Then keep your attention on your normal breathing. If you notice you start thinking about something else, just bring your attention back to your breath.

This is a simple breath meditation.

Extra Support

You can give your meditation practice extra support by adding an intention before you start and a dedication at the end.

Intention: Ask yourself why you are meditating. Your answer is your intention. It guides your practice. For example, you could say, "I meditate to understand myself and the world better," or "I meditate to feel my natural state."

Dedication: Dedicating your meditation is like sealing it with kindness. You could say, "I dedicate my meditation to kids like me who sometimes feel mad or sad." You could also dedicate your practice to your best friend or even to your pet. It's your choice.

This reminds you that you are part of a community of people who all want to be happy, just like you.

MINDFUL ME Questions and Answers

You might have a few more questions about mindfuless and meditation. Here are some that people often ask.

How long should I meditate?

This is up to you. Some people like to start with three minutes. Other people like to meditate longer—ten minutes, twenty minutes, even an hour or more. There is no magic number. Trust yourself to find the best amount of time.

Is mindfulness a religious practice?

Mindfulness is a method for you to pay attention to whatever is happening in the present moment. MINDFUL ME practices and activities do not belong to any specific religion.

Do I force myself not to think during meditation?

The mind thinks. That's one of its biggest jobs. In meditation, you do not need to struggle with your mind. Instead, just watch what it does, without reacting to it. Become curious about the way your mind works. You might discover that you have a very busy mind, or a very quiet mind. Explore it!

Does mindfulness mean I accept whatever happens to me, even bullying?

Being a MINDFUL ME means accepting yourself—with all of your thoughts and emotions—and the situations you face.

But let's be clear—being a MINDFUL ME **does not mean** you let others hurt you. Bullying is an unMINDFUL way of handling a social situation. You may not be able to stop a bully, but you can make healthy choices and stay safe.

MINDFUL ME PRACTICE is not enough if you are ever physically unsafe. In that case, please talk to an adult you trust. Self-care is a strong part of being a MINDFUL ME. Do not keep silent if you feel you are in danger.

What Is Self-Care?

Self-care means knowing what you need to be well, treating yourself with kindness, and taking positive actions to function well. For example, let's say you become cranky and frustrated when you don't get enough sleep. When you practice self-care, you could choose to go to bed early enough to sleep well and wake up refreshed. That way, you don't start off the day in a bad mood.

Here's another example. Let's say you have a peanut or other food allergy. If someone offers you a food that will make you sick, you politely explain you cannot eat it. This is especially important if you have a health condition that other people may not understand. You speak up for yourself to stay healthy. That is self-care.

Self-care is very important if someone is hurting you, either with words or physical contact. Move away from the situation when you can, and ask someone you trust for help.

Self-care is not the same as being *selfish*, which means focusing on yourself without thinking of others. With self-care, you realize you are an equal and important part of a community, and so is everyone else. That means you treat yourself well so that you are in good shape to be a friend, classmate, family member, or community participant.

MINDFUL ME Practice Tips

• You may want to set a timer with a gentle ringtone for your meditation sessions. Increase your meditation time as you strengthen your practice.

• If you feel bored during meditation, explore how boredom feels in your body. Can you be comfortable doing nothing? If not, ask yourself why not.

• If your mind hops around from one thought to the next, no worries. You don't have to fix it. Let it be. Gradually you may find you can focus your mind more on the object of your meditation.

• If you feel wiggly during meditation, alternate sitting and moving meditation.

• If your body is a little uncomfortable during meditation, notice the discomfort before you adjust yourself. Feel the itch before you scratch. This trains your mind not to react immediately. If you feel strong pain, stop your meditation and talk to an adult who can help you. Asking for help is part of self-care.

- If sitting silently with your eyes closed scares you, open your eyes and focus on something in front of you. If that does not help, talk to someone you trust about feeling scared.

- If you start to fall asleep during meditation, shift your gaze higher and take full breaths. If that does not help, take a nap and meditate later.

- With MINDFUL ME movement, do not push yourself if something is not comfortable. Choose a modification if it feels better.

- Self-care is **always** important in MINDFUL ME PRACTICE.

- MINDFUL ME PRACTICE is about being aware and open. It is not about being good or bad, right or wrong, better or worse. MINDFUL ME PRACTICE is never competitive.

Modifications

Anyone can practice mindfulness. Your body need not limit you. Make whatever modifications are right for you. If you use special equipment to sit or move, feel free to incorporate it into your practice. You could also use your mind to visualize a movement activity. The idea is to pay attention to whatever you are experiencing in the present moment.

What's Your MINDFUL ME Style?

Some people love a crowd and are great at bringing a group together. Others are happiest reading a book, painting, or bird-watching on a nature trail. How well do you know yourself? Answer these questions to find out your MINDFUL ME style—Sun, Moon, Wind, or Fire. You might even discover you're a combination of two. Then look for the activities that best suit you.

Take this quiz. How would you act in these situations?

1. When you have free time, you would rather:
   A. organize an activity with friends.
   B. read a book or play an electronic game alone.
   C. play guitar in a band or build a robot
      with a team of kids.
   D. run for student government.

2. If you have to sit quietly and wait in a room by yourself, you:
   A. do your homework.
   B. daydream.
   C. fidget or bounce your legs up and down.
   D. pace around the room.

3. Your friend is telling you a long story. You:
    A. show enthusiasm and keep the conversation going.
    B. feel overwhelmed and wish for quiet.
    C. listen carefully and ask specific questions.
    D. interrupt and talk about yourself.

4. You have an important test tomorrow. You:
    A. review your class notes with a study group.
    B. close yourself into a room with your textbook.
    C. put on headphones, listen to music, and write out a practice answer.
    D. study for ten minutes, check social media, talk with friends, study some more.

5. Your class is putting on a play. You:
    A. try out for the lead.
    B. work backstage.
    C. write the play.
    D. direct the play.

Turn the page to see your answers.

What's Your MINDFUL ME Style? Answers

SUN

If you chose mostly *A* answers, you're usually outgoing and upbeat, and you tend to like a crowd. You may be a leader with loads of ideas. It's great you have energy and a positive nature, but remember not everyone's like you. Some people would rather stand in the shade. Notice how your actions affect others, and give them a chance to shine too. You can be a great friend.

Suggested MINDFUL ME activities: **Jigsaw Puzzle, I Hear You, Heart-Happy**

MOON

If you chose mostly *B* answers, you may be a quiet or shy person who prefers to be alone rather than in a crowd. You could be sensitive and creative, and you may like to think up special projects for yourself. You have strength in your independence, but remember to ask for help when you need it. Other people might not understand who you are unless you tell them. And when you do, they will be amazed.

Suggested MINDFUL ME activities: **Cloud Floating, MINDFUL ME Tasting**

WIND

 If you chose mostly C answers, you may be great at creative projects and inspiring others. You have strong beliefs and let people know your opinions. You could be touchy if things don't go your way, so watch that you don't cause a storm. You are a strong leader, but you might choose to recharge on your own.

Suggested MINDFUL ME activities: **Special Place, Challenge Your Thoughts**

FIRE

 If you chose mostly D answers, you may be full of energy and emotion. You love being part of the gang and can stir up fun. You react strongly to life, so be careful you don't burn out. Understanding how to respond to your emotions could be a big plus. Let your WISDOM MIND blaze.

Suggested MINDFUL ME activities: **Find the Gap, MINDFUL ME Moving**

Chapter 2
MINDFUL ME Inner Self

When Life Feels Crazy

Sometimes life gets crazy. There are school, sports practice, music lessons, family chores, homework, and the list goes on and on. You are so busy, busy, busy that you often don't realize what you are feeling or thinking. You might not notice what's happening to the people around you. You forget to talk to your friends or you ignore your siblings. You might even feel like there's a weight on your shoulders, and you become grumpy without realizing why.

That's the perfect time to take a short break, try a MINDFUL ME meditation exercise, and relax.

Meditation is like a personal pause button. It lets you focus your attention, open your heart, and listen to your *WISDOM MIND*.

What is your WISDOM MIND? It's your inner intuition. It's always there, even when you are upset or don't believe in yourself. Even when life feels really hard.

This chapter offers meditation exercises and visualizations to help you connect to your WISDOM MIND. Let's try some.

Who Am I?

The minute you are born, people talk about you. "Oh, what a cute baby," they might say. So that makes you cute. Later people make comments about you—kind or unkind—and they stick to you. Labels like smart. Pretty.

Weird. Fat. Skinny. Athletic. Nerdy. You know all about labels and reputations. They're hard to change.

Before you know it, you might believe a label that someone else gave you. Or, you spend time saying, "Those labels aren't true, and I can prove it." All those labels and judgments—positive or negative—become part of you. What can you do about it?

What if you question them to see if they're true? Even better, what if you let all of them go? Don't believe a single one. Would you feel strange without any labels? What if you could dig deeper and find out who you really are? Not what other people say you are.

Let's try a visualization to do that. Read the next section, and then meditate on it or ask someone to read it aloud while you meditate.

Jigsaw Puzzle

Sometimes you let other people define you, but that might cause you to feel mixed up. Try this visualization meditation to see who you really are without any labels.

Begin by sitting in MINDFUL ME POSTURE. Focus your eyes on a spot in front of you (or close them), and take three MINDFUL ME BREATHS. Allow your body to settle and relax.

Imagine you are a jigsaw puzzle made up of hundreds of pieces. Each piece is a judgment or label you have about yourself, or a label someone has given you. Breathe deeply, and see the jigsaw puzzle in your mind.

Next, take a few pieces away from the puzzle, and feel air pass through the empty space. Are *you* still there when pieces are missing? Give yourself time to *feel* the answer to this question in your heart.

Now, imagine all the puzzle pieces crumbling into dust. Where are you now? Breathe into the empty space around you. What is that like?

Can you feel your *inner* self still there? It might feel like empty space guiding you without words. Or like fresh air flowing through you. This is your WISDOM MIND. Can you connect to it for a few minutes? Take your time.

Now, when you are ready, shift your attention back to the room where you are sitting. Take three more MINDFUL ME BREATHS, and notice any sensations you are having in your body. Has anything shifted?

Allow yourself some time before you jump back into activity. You can choose to take your refreshed awareness with you.

Special Place

Relaxation meditations help you feel happy and more resilient so you can bounce back after a challenge. They could also increase your mental strength and concentration. Try this one to unwind and focus.

Begin by lying on a mat or blanket. Take three MINDFUL ME BREATHS, and close your eyes if you are comfortable doing so. Notice any sensations you are having in your body. With each breath, relax all your muscles.

Now, imagine you are in a special place, a place where you feel happy and safe. Use your imagination and see that place clearly. You might be at a beach or playground. You might be on a mountaintop or a Ferris wheel. Perhaps you have been there before, and you are remembering its details. Or perhaps you are creating a new special place in your mind.

Imagine looking up at the wide sky in your special place. Your WISDOM MIND is like this sky. Let the openness of the sky fill you. Take as long as you need. Breathe in the relaxation you feel in your special place. Notice what happens in your body when you feel happy. Soak it in.

When you are done, open your eyes and focus again on your body and breath. Do you notice any new sensations? Follow your breath as it comes in and goes out of your lungs.

Slowly return to your activity. You can bring your clear, open WISDOM MIND awareness with you now.

You can also draw a picture of your special place in your MINDFUL ME Activity Book or in your personal MINDFUL ME binder, if you wish. Put a note on your drawing about what was happening to you before your meditation, and date it. The next time you visit your special place, notice how things might be different.

Life's Flow

One part of MINDFUL ME PRACTICE is to become comfortable with life's constant flow and changes.

For a simple exercise, ask a parent or guardian to go on a mindfulness walk with you. Go around your backyard, around the block, through a park, in your neighborhood, or anywhere safe and convenient.

As you go in one direction, notice everything around you. Notice the weather and the sky. Look at the color of the trees or plants. If you're in the city, notice the colors of the buildings and signs. Do you see birds or insects? Do you see pets or squirrels? What are the people around you doing? Just notice, with present-moment awareness.

If you start thinking about something that happened yesterday or will happen tomorrow, check yourself and say, "I am only watching what is around me NOW."

Turn around and head back home. Go the same route if you can, and notice what has changed. Is the weather different? Has the sun shifted? Perhaps you took an evening stroll, and it is darker now. Perhaps more people have come out, or more have gone. Perhaps birds have flown away. Perhaps you are hungrier or more tired now than you were before.

This is a simple exercise, but sometimes doing something simple takes your mind off something hard. Go out for the same walk on another day, and look for more changes. Perhaps a tree has dropped its leaves, or a street has a new sign. Just as these external things keep changing, so too do you change. One day you feel sad, and another day you feel happy. Nothing stays the same.

Journal Prompts

Who Am I?

How would you define yourself? Are you comfortable with who you are? Why or why not? Would you like to change anything about yourself?

Mixed Up

Do you ever feel mixed up? What happens when you have this feeling?

Life's Flow

Did something change in your life that made you happy or unhappy? Write about it.

Comfortable Environment

Where do you feel most comfortable? Do you ever feel uncomfortable going someplace? What happens?

Getting to Know You

What is something you want people to know about you, but are afraid to tell them?

True to You

What are your favorite things to do? What are your least favorite things to do? Why?

Chapter 3
MINDFUL ME Emotions

Emotions Are Natural

We all know what it's like to feel an emotion. The whir of excitement when summer vacation begins. The sadness of a friend moving away. The guilt of cheating on a test. The pride of getting a good grade on an assignment. But what *are* emotions?

Emotions are internal reactions to our experiences. On the downside, emotions can push us to argue, fight, cheat, steal, and hurt ourselves or other people. On the upside, they motivate us to try new activities, take adventures, throw parties, invent cool things, lead social movements, and save lives. They also help us understand our values by showing us when we feel positive about something and when we don't.

Although emotions are natural, they sometimes feel uncomfortable in your body. People can feel different emotions about the same situation, and they express those emotions in various ways. For example, let's say you are invited to a party at an amusement park, and all the kids have tickets to the roller-coaster ride. Some kids are happy and excited, and they jump around until they can climb aboard the car. Other kids may feel anxious and upset about riding the roller-coaster, and even embarrassed about not wanting to go on the ride. They may stop talking, cross their arms over the chest, or walk away because of fear. People have different realities of the same experience.

Emotions often cause different physical reactions too. You can use MINDFUL ME PRACTICE to help you understand the emotions you feel and the ways you express them physically.

Here are some examples of emotions and the ways people express them through body language.

Examples of Emotions

Sad	Guilty	Hopeless
Happy	Confident	Hopeful
Mad	Scared	Ashamed
Content	Brave	Honored
Frustrated	Confused	Envious
Excited	Proud	Compassionate
Nervous	Bored	Depressed
Eager	Grateful	Cheerful

Emotions Expressed through Body Language

Happiness: You may feel relaxed with loose muscles and open body language. You may smile, laugh, jump around, dance, sing, or even swing your arms.

Excitement: Maybe you jump up and down, grin, talk fast, bounce your legs up and down when you're sitting, feel jittery, and talk fast or loudly. Your heart may beat very fast. Your hands may feel sweaty.

Fear: You may sweat, avoid eye contact, tremble, tense up, hold your breath, cross your arms over your body, freeze in place, or bite your lip or fingernails.

Sadness: You may feel heavy in your chest, curl up in a ball, have trouble talking, get teary, cry, sniffle, have an upset stomach, hunch over, or avoid people.

Anger: You may get red in the face, clench your fists, grit your teeth, lower your eyebrows, press your lips together, tense your muscles, or feel an urge in your legs to run or in your hands to hit. Your heart may pound hard and fast.

Worry: Maybe you fidget, bite your lip, hunch your shoulders, laugh nervously, breathe fast, chew on a pen or pencil, or feel an urge to eat even if you're not hungry.

Surprise: You may gasp, open your eyes wide, open your mouth, raise your eyebrows, tense your muscles, or step backward.

Embarrassment: Your neck or face may turn red. You may look down or away from people, make a tight smile, have a fluttery feeling in your stomach, mumble, or talk fast.

Working with Emotions

Now that we're talking about emotions and how we feel and express them physically, let's dive into some MINDFUL ME exercises that could increase your awareness of emotions. Understanding them will help you work with them.

BFF—Breathe, Focus, Feel

When you feel worked up and full of emotions, think **B F F—Breathe, Focus, and Feel.** You can do this easy exercise anytime, anywhere, as a way to become aware of your inner experience of emotions.

Breathe—Stop whatever you are doing, and notice your breathing. Are you taking quick or slow breaths? Are they shallow or deep? Now add three soft, slow MINDFUL ME BREATHS. Give them your full attention. Notice the air as it comes in through your nose or mouth. Notice where it goes. Does it fill your chest or expand your belly? Notice the change when you feel your breath go out.

Focus—Shift your attention from your breath to your physical sensations. Does anything ache, itch, or throb? Is anything tight or uncomfortable? Have you been ignoring a headache or cramp in your belly? Just notice whatever you are experiencing. You can choose to relax your muscles if they feel tight. Notice if that changes anything you feel physically.

Feel your feet on the floor. Notice how they anchor you to the ground. If you are sitting, feel contact with your seat. Feel the air on your skin. Feel your heartbeat in your chest.

By **BFF**—breathing, focusing, and feeling—you give yourself the chance to connect to your WISDOM MIND before you act on any emotion.

Holding the Heat

Sometimes we burn with anger and can't release it. Anger is emotional energy in the body, and you can work with it by holding it safe instead of reacting to it.

When you are mad and want to calm down, start by standing still and taking three MINDFUL ME BREATHS. Rub your hands together until you feel heat. Then hold your palms in front of you and imagine you are holding a ball of this heat. The ball is the energy of your anger.

Breathe in, pull your hands apart a little bit, and imagine the ball expanding. Breathe out and see it contract. Your hands move in and out as you breathe. You can rub your hands together again when you want to feel more heat.

Stand with this ball of heat for as long as you are comfortable. Feel its energy. If you keep it safe between your hands, it won't hurt you or anyone else.

When you have finished this exercise, shake out your hands to release any leftover tension. By now, some of your emotional energy may have dispersed, and you may feel calmer or more willing to talk about your anger with someone you trust.

Hold and Release

When you are upset or busy, you may not realize how tight your muscles have become. When your muscles are tight, your mind might feel tight too.

This exercise could help you relax deeply. It's useful any time you want to unwind and calm down. Try it before going to sleep too.

Find a quiet room, and lie on your back on a mat or blanket. You can also lie on your bed. Watch the rise and fall of your belly during three MINDFUL ME BREATHS.

Let your attention go to your feet. Wiggle your toes a little. Now tighten your foot muscles and hold. Then release and feel your muscles relax.

Move your attention up to your legs. Squeeze your leg muscles really tight and hold, hold, hold. Then relax.

Slowly tighten, hold, and release all the muscles from your toes to the top of your head. Focus on the muscles in your hips, your belly, your arms, your shoulders, your neck, your jaw, your face, your eyes, even your eyebrows and the crown of your head. Go slowly, and focus on one group of muscles at a time.

Hold and release. Hold and release.

When you finish, notice all your muscles softening like melting ice cream. Rest your body for as long as you wish before ending this exercise.

If you want to sleep now, let yourself drift off. Otherwise, you can take your relaxation with you when you finish. If you are on a floor or the ground, roll to your side and stand up slowly.

Pain or Problem

Sometimes when you feel emotional or stressed, your body reacts with pain or discomfort. You may make this discomfort worse by fighting it, hiding it, or worrying too much about it.

We often ignore pain when it's telling us an important message about our health and well-being. Always check out your pain. Tell a helpful adult when something hurts. After you know what's going on, try this meditation to help you deal with your pain or discomfort.

Pain or Problem Meditation

Sit in MINDFUL ME POSTURE, and allow your attention to go to the physical sensations you have in your body. Feel your seat where you make contact with your cushion. Feel air going in and out of your nose or mouth. Notice if you are uncomfortable anywhere.

If you feel pain or discomfort, ask yourself what kind of sensation it is. Does it itch? Is it achy or hot? Is it sharp? Does it come and go? Can you squeeze and relax the muscles around your discomfort?

Now notice your mind. Are you complaining about the sensation? Worrying? Do your thoughts make it worse or better? Just notice your thoughts, and then return to paying attention to physical sensations.

Be curious about them. Do the sensations change when you focus on them? Sometimes an itch will fade away. Sometimes an ache will ease when you relax your muscles and slow your breathing.

Just keep noticing.

When you are ready to end this meditation, take three MINDFUL ME BREATHS, noticing your in breath and out breath.

You can bring this type of awareness with you for the rest of your day.

Journal Prompts

Feeling Emotions

When you have a strong emotion like anger or fear, where do you feel it? Describe what happens.

Habits

Do you have any physical habits like biting your fingernails, bouncing your legs up and down when you're sitting, or chewing your lip? What emotions trigger this habit? Does the habit soothe you or make you feel worse?

Working with Emotions

Describe what happens when you work with your emotions through MINDFUL ME exercises. Do you notice your emotions or physical sensations shifting? Are some emotions really stubborn?

Favorite Feelings

What is your favorite and least favorite emotion to experience and why? How do they make you feel inside?

Understanding Difficult Feelings

Describe a time when you felt a strong emotion that was uncomfortable. What triggered it, and what happened? Would you handle the situation differently now?

Chapter 4
MINDFUL ME Thoughts

The Mind's Control Tower

Your mind can be like a busy airport, your thoughts coming in and taking off like planes. Some planes circle the runway, just like thoughts. If you let them fly wild, you may never feel peaceful.

But you are in the control tower. When something bothers you, and you can't stop thinking about it, you could try a few methods to work with your thoughts.

First, you could start an activity that requires mental focus, such as playing chess, practicing an instrument, or playing a game with friends. These might take your mind off whatever was troubling you. You might discover that you've forgotten your problem or that your past thoughts no longer seem like such a big deal.

Second, you could practice MINDFUL ME meditation and focus your mind on your breathing or on a visualization. This is a powerful way to break the chain of a persistent thought.

Third, you could challenge or replace your thoughts. Sometimes thoughts are so strong that you believe them without questioning them. If you take time to challenge your thoughts, you may discover they are not as true or important as you believed.

Working with your thoughts is a good way to keep them from hurting you. How do thoughts hurt you? They often make you feel worse or provoke you to do something you will regret.

Here's an example of how this happens.

Thoughts That Hurt You

Imagine you see a group of kids playing a game together. Two of your close friends are in the group. You walk by, and nobody asks you to join the game.

What would you think? Would you feel hurt that nobody included you? Would you start thinking mean things about the other kids, especially your two close friends? Would you start feeling bad about yourself?

Perhaps you'd think there is something wrong with you because the kids didn't invite you in. "I am no good at games, so they didn't want me to play." Or, "Those kids don't like me."

The next time you see your friends who were playing with the group, you might think, "They don't like me anymore, so I'm not going to say hello."

These negative thoughts might make you feel terrible. Because you feel this way, you might do something unhelpful to get rid of your uncomfortable feeling. Maybe you break something. Maybe you kick something hard and hurt your toes. Maybe you spread a mean rumor about your friends.

Now is the time to stop before you make things worse. Ask yourself if you are giving your thoughts too much power over you.

Challenge Your Thoughts

When a thought keeps bothering you, ask yourself the following questions. Afterward, decide if you need to respond to the thought.

Questions to Challenge Your Thoughts

- What is the negative thought in my mind that won't go away?
- How does it make me feel?
- Is this thought *really* true?
- How do I know it's true?
- What would happen if it *were* true?
- If that happens, how would I feel and respond?
- Is it possible that my thought is *not* true?
- What would change if I didn't believe this thought?
- Could I watch my thought without reacting to it?
- Could I replace this thought with a positive thought?
- What is different if I believe the positive thought instead of the negative thought?
- Could I talk out my thought with someone I trust?

After you have challenged your thoughts, decide if you need help to talk something out. If you are still working things out on your own, you can take the next step to replace negative thoughts.

Replacing Negative Thoughts

Too much negative thinking can hurt your health. It can also hurt your relationships with friends and family. Try turning negative thoughts into positive ones.

Can you spot a negative thought in your mind and replace it with a positive one? See what happens when you do that. It may take practice, but over time you could find yourself thinking more positively.

In your journal, draw the chart below and fill it in with your own examples of negative thoughts that you replace with positive thoughts.

Negative Thoughts	Positive Thoughts
I'm no good at anything.	I always do the best I can.
I don't fit in because of the way I look.	There's only one me— I am unique.
People think I'm weird.	I am comfortable being myself.
I failed.	I can learn from my mistakes.
School is hard.	Challenges help me grow.
I don't like people who are different from me.	It's fun to learn from people with different customs.

What Do I Tell Myself?

Sometimes, you try something new and you fail. Then you may tell yourself things like "I'm stupid. I never should have tried that" or "I'll never be good at that." This kind of thinking can bring you down.

Other times you may look at yourself in the mirror and not like what you see because it does not fit an image you see in a magazine or on social media. You might think, "My face is too chubby," or "My clothes aren't cool enough." This inner dialogue of judging and comparing might be running through your mind without you even realizing. It can be hurtful.

Your thoughts are your brain's way of talking to you. But do you notice the kinds of messages you are giving yourself? Do you say supportive things that make you feel great like "Keep trying. You'll get better and better." Or do you say unhelp- ful or mean things to yourself that you would never say to a friend like, "You look terrible!" Negative thinking is stressful, and it can affect your mood and health.

Throughout the day, notice what you say to yourself in your mind. In your MINDFUL ME Activity Book or binder, keep track of the words or phrases you use often. You can put them in categories:

What I Say to Myself:

Helpful

Friendly

Supportive

Silly

Mean

Critical

Working with Your Mind

After you notice and write down the thoughts you have in your head, you can start working with them. You will be amazed at the many ways you can train your mind.

Your mind is flexible and changeable—the scientific word for that is *neuroplastic*—and your brain cells can adjust to new situations and changes in your environment. That means the more you work with your mind in a positive way, the more benefits you may feel. Just because you have a habit now of getting angry easily, or being negative toward yourself, or being super shy does not mean you will always be that way. The good news is people can and do change, if they work at it.

Try the following exercises and visualizations to train your mind.

Mind Drawing

Have you ever noticed your mind wandering when you want to focus on something? Perhaps you checked social media for messages when you were doing homework, or you stared out the window in class and missed what the teacher was saying.

You can try a MINDFUL ME method to help you develop your mental focus and concentration. This mind-drawing meditation may help, if you practice it often.

Begin by sitting in MINDFUL ME POSTURE and taking three MINDFUL ME BREATHS.

Think of something you enjoy looking at. It can be as small as a flower or as large as a castle. Take some time to draw it with your mind. Add details and color and definition.

If your mind wanders, pretend your thoughts are bubbles and *pop* them. Then, go back to your drawing.

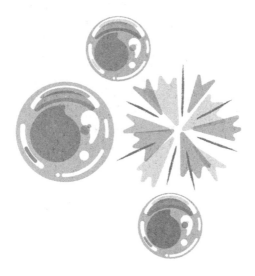

When your mind drawing is finished, examine it.

If it's small, imagine holding it. Notice its shape and texture.

If it is large like a castle, imagine standing next to it or walking through it. What do you see that you didn't notice before?

Give yourself some time with this exercise. If you become distracted and lose your drawing in your mind, start over at any point. You may have to begin drawing again several times. That's okay. With practice, you will develop concentration.

When you're ready, breathe in and out slowly and shift your attention back to the room where you are. You can bring your mental focus with you.

Mind Clearing

Fighting or pushing away your thoughts might make you feel worse because you have a battle going on in your mind. Instead, notice your thoughts, give them your full attention, and then practice accepting and releasing them by using a visualization.

Begin by sitting in a MINDFUL ME POSTURE and taking three MINDFUL ME BREATHS.

Notice the thoughts you are thinking right now. Do they seem connected to strong emotions you feel? Allow yourself a little time to notice what is going on. You do not need to judge yourself for having certain thoughts, even if they don't seem pleasant. With kindness, accept yourself with all of your experiences. Having strong thoughts and emotions is part of being human.

When you understand what you are thinking and feeling and are ready to work with your mind, start with this visualization.

Imagine a glowing ball of white light at the top of your head. Give it the power of kindness and compassion. See the white light expand and pour down into your head and body. You are filling up with white light.

Now imagine your thoughts and feelings—anything that confuses or upsets you—as gray smoke. Breathe in, and feel the white light moving down inside you.

Breathe out, and imagine the gray smoke going out of your mouth, nose, and ears. The smoke vanishes into the space around you.

Let your mind rest on the white light inside you. Imagine it giving you a freshness. You have released whatever was blocking you into the gray smoke.

Sit in quiet meditation for as long as you like.

When you are ready, focus your eyes back in the room. Return to your regular activity when you're ready. You can take the white light with you, if you wish.

Mind Safe

This activity is helpful if you have a worry or fear that won't go away. Take an old box and label it "Mind Safe." A safe is a locked box where people store their treasures. You might not have a real safe, but you can create something that will do the job. Decorate your Mind Safe in any way you like. If you don't have a box, use a drawer.

Write down your worry or fear on a piece of paper, and slip it into the box. It is safe there. You don't need to carry it around in your mind anymore. You don't need to go to sleep with this worry.

You can check your box whenever you wish. You can share your worry with an adult you trust. Sometimes, you may discover that the worry is no longer important, or you have resolved whatever issue worried you.

Bonus: You might want to create a *Joy Box* too. Every time something makes you happy or joyful, write it down on a slip of paper. Drop the paper into your Joy Box. Someday you may want to explore the contents of both boxes side by side. That would give you a good idea of how you have been feeling.

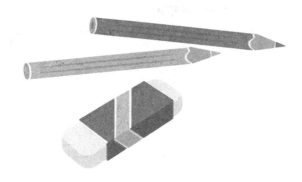

Color Your Thoughts

Another way to notice how your thinking affects your emotions is by examining thoughts closely and putting them into emotional categories.

Take a few moments to write down everything you are thinking RIGHT NOW. Don't judge yourself; just write. Keep writing freely until you run out of thoughts.

Then, with colored pencils or markers, put your thoughts into color categories. You can choose whatever colors you want for your categories, but here is an example:

CIRCLE all of your...

Angry thoughts in **red**

Fearful thoughts in **yellow**

Critical or judgmental thoughts in **green**

Excited thoughts in **orange**

Happy thoughts in **blue**

Neutral thoughts in **purple**

Now count each colored group of circles. How many reds? How many blues? And so on. This will help you understand what is going on in your mind. Do you have more angry thoughts today? Or, maybe you're excited and all your thoughts are circled in orange.

Don't worry if you have many thoughts in one color. It's okay to have these thoughts. Tomorrow, your color patterns might look different. Remember, you are learning to work with your mind.

Now that you have put your thoughts into categories, do you notice how they are connected to your emotions? Did you realize you were feeling happy or excited or simply neutral today?

Try this exercise again another day, and see how your thoughts are different. You could also use a calendar and mark each day with the color of your first thought when you wake up or your last thought when you go to bed. Check back at the end of the week, and see how your thoughts affected your emotions over time.

Journal Prompts

Mind Grip

What is always on your mind that won't go away? Is this a helpful thought? Why or why not?

Negative to Positive

Pick one negative thought you have. How can you change it into a positive thought?

Thoughts and Emotions

Have you noticed how your thoughts and emotions are connected? Explain how.

Happy Secret

Are you a happy person with happy thoughts? What is the secret to your happy mind?

Criticism to Support

Do you ever criticize yourself in your mind? What do you say? What steps do you take to turn self-criticism into self-support?

Chapter 5
MINDFUL ME Actions

Connecting the Dots

In the last two chapters, we talked about working with your emotions and your thoughts. In this chapter, we take the conversation further by showing how emotions, thoughts, and *actions* are all connected.

When you **feel** happy, you often **think** positive thoughts. You probably **act** friendly and smile. You may even jump around with joy or call a friend to do something fun.

But when you **feel** unhappy, you often **think** negative thoughts, and you might **act** out by yelling, sulking, hiding, or slamming a door.

That's probably obvious, right?

But sometimes you don't know exactly what's bugging you, and you don't realize what you're doing. You may say things you don't mean or do things you regret later. Then you ask yourself, "Why did I do that?"

Through MINDFUL ME PRACTICE, you learn how your emotions, thoughts, and physical sensations are connected. Let's say you are playing a game with a group of kids after school, and you never get a turn. Nobody else notices, and they keep playing, running around and having fun.

You **feel** hurt. You **think** everyone is mean. You *react* by shouting and walking away mad. The other kids don't know why you got angry and left. Now they are upset with *you*.

Then you see your little brother (or sister) at home. He's excited you're home and wants to play with you. You're so mad that you push him aside and lock yourself in your room. Your little brother starts crying because he doesn't know why you treated him like that. He just wanted to play with you. He's upset. You're upset. That's how bad feelings spread.

You sit alone in your room, and you can't stop thinking about the unfair game. You don't even realize how your brother is feeling now. You feel so frustrated that your stomach starts to ache, and you don't want dinner. You can't focus on your homework, and your teacher is annoyed when you have nothing to turn in the next day. Your friends are still confused about your frustration and don't talk to you.

This example shows how one unpleasant event can start a chain reaction of negative thoughts, emotions, and actions. If only you knew how to catch yourself when you're upset *before* you do something you'll regret!

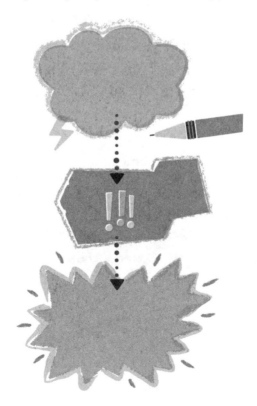

With MINDFUL ME PRACTICE, you can learn to interrupt this chain of negative reactions. You do this by **Connecting the Dots** between your physical sensations, emotions, and thoughts, and then by adding a simple exercise called **Finding the Gap** before you take any action.

Here's how it works:

1. Something happens, and you feel upset. The situation has *hooked* you, and you want to react by getting mad, or crying, or saying something mean. Instead of reacting, pay attention to your physical sensations, which could give you clues about the emotions you are feeling. Connect the dots between your sensations and emotions.

2. You may have strong thoughts too, which give power to your emotions. Notice your thoughts. You could put them into colored categories as we did in the last chapter, if that helps you see what you're telling yourself. Connect the dots between your thoughts and emotions.

3. Now practice **Finding the Gap**.

Finding the Gap

This breathing meditation helps you see how things shift and change moment to moment—even your thoughts and emotions. When you notice the natural pauses or gaps in your breathing, you can often experience the silent space between thoughts. That is where you experience the present-moment awareness of your WISDOM MIND. In that gap, your mind is not reflecting on the past or planning for the future. Instead, it rests in the open awareness of **NOW**.

Begin by sitting in a MINDFUL ME POSTURE and taking three MINDFUL ME BREATHS. If you are breathing fast and shallow breaths because you are upset, see if they slow down when you become fully aware of your breathing.

When your breathing steadies, notice that at the end of each out breath there is a little pause or gap before you breath in again. Each time you breath out, focus your attention on that gap in your breathing. It might also feel like a pause in your thinking or a silent space.

Breathe in again. Breathe out, and feel the gap.

Sit in meditation for as long as you like, finding those gaps at the end of your out breath.

When you are ready, perhaps feeling less hooked by emotion, end your meditation and move on to the next steps.

4. **Think** ahead and ask yourself: What is my best response to this conflict so I don't do something I'll regret? Think of some options.

5. **See** the consequences of those options. If the consequences are not helpful, perhaps you're not ready to respond. Take another step.

6. **Practice** another MINDFUL ME technique. Any one that helps you. Connect to your WISDOM MIND inside.

7. **Respond** to the conflict situation when you can act with patience and self-care, or wait until you are in a better frame of mind. Sometimes the best response is *no* response. Other times the best response is to listen to the other people in the conflict as they tell you how they saw the situation. That could help you see the whole picture—both your side and theirs.

Going through this process helps you to accept whatever you are experiencing and choose the best response. Your feelings might change in an hour or a day. The more you practice taking these steps, the easier the process will be. It may become automatic, so you are always thoughtful during conflicts.

Scene Replay

Remember that imaginary scene when you were mad at your friends and then mean to your brother? Let's look at that scene when we add steps for **Connecting the Dots** and **Finding the Gap**.

You're playing the game, and you haven't had a turn. You start to feel upset, your face feels hot, and you want to cry and yell at the same time. In your mind, you connect the dots between your thoughts, emotions, and physical sensations.

You take three MINDFUL ME BREATHS to steady yourself, and you ask for what you need. You interrupt the game to talk to your friends, and you explain that you haven't had a turn yet. You tell them you want to join in, and you ask to have a turn like everyone else. Maybe the other kids didn't notice they skipped you, and now they give you a turn. Great. Everyone is more aware now.

Or, perhaps the other kids still ignore you, and you check in with your **feelings** again. You're hurt. You know you're angry too because your face is hot and you're clenching your teeth. You notice you are **thinking** unkind things about the other kids, and you want to yell at them. Accept whatever thoughts and emotions you are having, but choose to react to them mindfully.

Before you **act**, pay attention to your breathing, finding the gap at the end of each out breath. This could give you a little time to experience present-moment awareness and your WISDOM MIND. You could respond in a more positive way.

Here is the moment you give yourself power. Ask yourself, "Where will yelling and hitting get me?" (In trouble, probably.)

So, choose a MINDFUL ME **response** instead.

You tell the others that you won't play if nobody will give you a turn, but that you will come back when the game is fair. You walk away with the confidence that you have chosen the best response at the time.

When your little brother wants to play with you at home, you remember what it feels like not to be included. You stop and play with him. He's happy, and you feel better because you did something kind for him. You eat dinner with your family and let them support you. Maybe you talk about the situation and ask your family for advice. Your little brother tells you, "You have to take turns, or it's not fair." He's right, but we all forget sometimes.

You tell him, "Tomorrow, let's play catch after school."

Congratulations!

In the second version of the scene, you took control of your response to conflict, even though you had strong feelings. You weren't a victim. Perhaps the game didn't turn out the way you wanted, but you responded in a way that didn't make you miserable. There was no negative chain reaction. And perhaps you learned something helpful about how you respond best to situations that upset you.

Remember, you can't control circumstances or other people. You can only control how you respond.

Accepting Your Inner Experiences

The more you understand and accept yourself with kindness and compassion, the easier you will be able to handle your inner experiences. Acceptance doesn't always happen smoothly, though. You might have to remind yourself frequently that having emotions and thoughts is normal. Little by little, you will learn not to *react* to them but to *respond* wisely to the situation that triggered them.

But what if you've been practicing this regularly, and you still feel you are reacting to things? If that's the case, you may need to give yourself a break. Let it all go, just for a time. Try **Cloud Floating** for deep relaxation.

Giving Yourself a Break

Cloud Floating

In this exercise, you do nothing but take a mindful rest.

Start by lying down on a mat, blanket, or bed and taking three MINDFUL ME BREATHS. Then close your eyes if you like. If not, keep them open slightly, and look at a spot above you.

Imagine you are lying on a fluffy white cloud. It lifts you off the ground and into the sky. You are free to float and relax. Let your body and mind sink into the cloud. You can notice your breath coming in and going out, if you wish.

If a thought or worry comes into your mind, acknowledge it is there. It is like a cloud in the sky floating past you. Clouds float near. Clouds float away. You don't need to do anything about them.

Relax this way for as long as you need. Breathe into the empty space around you.

When you are finished, you can thank yourself for taking some time to relax. When you are ready to end this session, roll to your side and get up slowly.

Bonus: You can also try this outside. Lie on the ground and watch the wide sky. Let your mind be as open as the sky.

Feeling Strong and Confident

Feeling relaxed could help you feel confident. Feeling confident could give you the boost you need to handle whatever situation arises. Another exercise that could help you feel empowered is **Be the Mountain**. It's easy and takes only a few minutes.

Be the Mountain

To start, find a place where you can have a moment to yourself. You could try your bedroom or a bathroom where you can stand in front of a mirror. Hold your arms open wide above your head to make yourself bigger. Imagine you are a tall mountain rising through the clouds. Between your arms is clear, open sky.

If you are standing in front of a mirror, look into your eyes. Feel your inner strength. Breathe in the sky. Stand this way for as long as you can. Go for two minutes, if you're up to it. You could even repeat to yourself, "Be the mountain. Be the mountain."

Be the Mountain

Feel strength rising up from the ground, through your feet, to the top of your head. Feel power in your extended arms and in your fingertips. Breathe MINDFUL ME BREATHS, and focus on the air coming in and going out of your nose or mouth.

When you are ready, lower your arms. Feel the strength in your beating heart.

Be the mountain!

Journal Prompts

Acting Out

Write about a time when you acted on your feelings without thinking first. How do you feel now about that situation?

Rewrite a Scene

Rewrite the same scene. Imagine taking time to connect the dots and find the gap before you act. What happens in the new scene?

Mind over Matter

There's a famous saying: "If you don't mind, it doesn't matter."

That means a situation doesn't matter if you choose not to let it bother you. For example, a mosquito bite might itch, but it's not a problem if you don't let it bother you. As another example, losing a game is not a crisis unless you make it one. Write about something that could bother you if you let it, but you choose not to. Explain why you don't mind at all.

Happy Inspiration

Think about a time when you were happy. Did your

mood inspire you to do something interesting? What happened?

Call to Action

Did you ever have to respond to a situation by thinking quickly and jumping into action? What happened?

Chapter 6
MINDFUL ME Heart

When you think of your heart, you may imagine the organ that pumps blood through your body. You need your heart to live.

You could also think of the heart as your emotional center. We use the heart symbol for happy things, or a broken heart for sad things. We put our hand over our heart to promise something, and "give" our heart to someone we love.

Your heart is involved in the activities you do and the emotions you feel. One way you can notice this connection is by feeling your heartbeat. It will change depending upon what you are doing and experiencing.

Let's try this out.

Heart Jumping

Sometimes your heart beats very fast when you are excited, nervous, or upset. You may not realize it if you are worked up, but your heart rate is a good measure of what is going on inside you.

This **heart-jumping exercise** helps you notice how your heartbeat changes with your activity and emotional state. Before you begin jumping, your heart rate might be slow—particularly if you have been sitting down and if you are feeling calm. After you jump for a minute or two, you can feel your heart beating faster.

Before you start, bring your hands to your chest and feel your heartbeat. If you can't feel it there, try finding your pulse on the inside of your wrist or on your neck, under your chin. Notice if the beat feels fast or slow. You can time your pulse by looking at a clock with a second hand or by using a timer. Count your heartbeats for thirty seconds. Double the number, and that's how many times your heart is beating per minute.

Now, start this exercise by standing with your feet hip-width apart. Feel the solid ground under your feet. Relax your shoulders and neck.

Next, hold your hands above your head, and bounce up and down on your toes for one or two minutes. For fun, bounce in a circle. Then go the other way. Add some jumping jacks and keep bouncing.

When your time is up, stop and feel your heartbeat again. Your heart is probably beating faster now than when you were seated. Take your pulse once more, if you wish. What do you notice?

Sit down again, and take twenty soft, slow MINDFUL ME BREATHS and feel your heartbeat a third time. What do you notice now?

This exercise is a good way to see how your heart rate changes.

Heartache

Heartache is part of life, but it doesn't feel good. It can come from grief, loneliness, or sadness.

Grief is a combination of feelings you have when someone you love dies or when your close circle of friends or family changes. You can also feel grief when your pet dies.

Sometimes you have to sit with your grief because it does not disappear easily or quickly. Trying to push grief away or cover it up does not usually work because you do not address the deep hurt inside you.

MINDFUL ME PRACTICE helps you accept your grief and sadness and understand how they affect you inside. The practice gives you ways to work with these emotions instead of acting out. Talking to people whom you love and trust is another important way to work with grief.

You could keep a journal on how you experience heartache and what steps you can take to address it. You can also use your MINDFUL ME Activity Book to keep track of your feelings.

Now that we know why we need to protect and strengthen our hearts, let's practice some new meditations.

Protection Circle

If your heart ever feels tender or insecure, try this meditation. You mentally protect yourself with wisdom and compassion. Compassion is even bigger than kindness. Compassion is having an understanding of the suffering of others and wanting to do something about it. You can develop compassion for yourself and for other people to build bonds.

When you're ready to meditate, begin by sitting in a MINDFUL ME POSTURE and taking three MINDFUL ME BREATHS.

Imagine a glowing ball of white light between your eyebrows. Give it the power of wisdom and compassion. Sit for a minute until you can see the light in your mind and feel wisdom and compassion in your heart.

Breathe out, and send that light out of your forehead and around your body. You are now in a circle of white light. Imagine it protecting you.

Now see a ball of red light inside your throat. Give it strength and courage. Breathe out, and send your red light all around you. You are doubly safe in circles of white and red light.

See blue light inside your heart. Empower the blue light with peace and calm to shield your MINDFUL ME heart. Breathe out, and send blue light around you.

Feel protected in three circles of light—white, red, and blue. Meditate there for several minutes.

Before you finish, visualize other people safe within their own three circles of light. Imagine saying to them, "May you be protected with wisdom and compassion, strength and courage, peace and calm." This step reminds you how everyone is connected by their need to feel wise, strong, peaceful, and safe.

End your meditation when you feel ready. You could take the feeling of protection with you as you carry on your day.

Sending Kindness

Friendship is another source of strength. When you show kindness to others, you make your own heart stronger while helping them. You can develop kindness through your everyday actions. You can also develop it by practicing this **Sending Kindness** meditation.

Start by sitting in a MINDFUL ME POSTURE and taking three MINDFUL ME BREATHS.

Think of someone you know who is kind to you. You could also think of your favorite pet. Notice how you feel happy around this person or animal.

Imagine that happy feeling inside you as a pulsing white light in your heart. It is the light of friendship and kindness. Fill yourself with it. Breathe it in.

Now think of another person who could use this friendship and kindness. Send white light from your heart to that person's heart. Imagine him or her receiving your light and feeling happy. Stay with the image for a moment or two.

Next, send your white light of friendship to someone you don't know well—or even someone you feel grumpy about. This might be a challenge, but try it. Imagine that person smiling with the kindness you send.

Now, send your white light of kindness to everyone in the world. See them smile. Feel the goodness spread across the planet.

Sit with the feeling for as long as you like. You can keep it with you, if you choose, when you close your meditation and carry on with your day.

Wise One

When you're stuck and don't know what to do, you can imagine yourself having a conversation with someone who *does* have the answers, your **wise one**.

Begin by sitting in a MINDFUL ME POSTURE and taking three MINDFUL ME BREATHS. Think about the situation that is causing you confusion. What question about it do you need answered? Take that question with you, and visit your wise one.

Imagine sitting in front of this very wise being. The wise one knows which choices you need to make to be happy.

Ask the question you brought with you, and let the wise one take time to reflect on it. You can take more MINDFUL ME BREATHS while you wait.

The wise one sends white light of wisdom into your heart to help you find the answer. Listen carefully when the wise one answers your question.

See yourself following this advice. Was it the right guidance you needed? If not, ask more questions until you know how to solve your problem.

Before you finish and get up, ask yourself, "Where did that wisdom come from?" You can always find the wise one inside you.

Happy List

When you become busy or upset, you often forget important happy parts of your life. You may not notice when a family member does something kind for you or when your best friend supports you. You may even forget you have nice clothes to wear, good food to eat, and a place to sleep. Many people do not have those things. And we often forget to feel grateful for them.

Each day, write down someone or something that makes you happy or grateful. It could be as small as

watching an ant crawling through the grass, or as big as making a new friend. Keep your **Happy List** in your MINDFUL ME Activity Book or in your binder.

If you're ever feeling down, go back and read your **Happy List.**

Heart-Happy Exercise

Sometimes you have a big dream. You may want to become a famous pop singer, an Olympic athlete, or a top chef. But you don't know how to accomplish your goal.

Did you know that if you visualize yourself achieving your goal, and then make a plan to achieve it, you have a better chance of success than if you sit back and wait for your dream to come true?

When you want to succeed, try this exercise:

Relax in a comfortable sitting position with paper and a pen in front of you, and take three MINDFUL ME BREATHS to focus your mind.

1. Think about what you want most in the world. Not something you can buy in a store. Something important to your deepest sense of who you are.

2. Imagine yourself accomplishing this goal. Take some time to do this. Maybe close your eyes and see all the details of this dream coming true. How do you feel inside when you imagine success?

3. Now, think about what obstacles inside yourself may be blocking your heart's desire. Write down whatever is in your way. These could be things like shyness, fear of failure, laziness, or a lack of skills.

4. This is the most important step: Ask yourself how you could overcome each obstacle. Write down

solutions to your challenges along the way. Write in if-then sentences:

If _____ (*obstacle*) is blocking me, then I will
_____ (*solution*).
If _____ (*obstacle*) is blocking me, then I will
_____ (*solution*).
If _____ (*obstacle*) is blocking me, then I will
_____ (*solution*).

Make a commitment to remove your obstacles one by one.

Helpful Hint: Sometimes we want something just because other people have it. Are you willing to make an effort to accomplish your heart's desire? If not, could you let this dream go and replace it with something else that fits you better? It's always your choice. Be true to yourself.

Example: I dream of playing violin in the school orchestra. When I imagine myself playing in the orchestra, I feel happy, inspired, and right where I am meant to be. So, I write down my if-then sentences to help me make a plan to accomplish my goals:

1. If I am not skilled enough at violin, I will ask a teacher to help me prepare for an audition. I will train until I am qualified to play in the orchestra.

2. If I am afraid of trying out, I will ask someone to help me set up an audition situation. I will perform for that person as if I am trying out for the orchestra. I will do this as many times as it takes me to feel more comfortable with the audition situation.

3. If I keep doubting my own ability and criticizing myself, I will question my thoughts and replace negative thinking with positive thinking.

Journal Prompts

Heartache

Have you experienced heartache or grief? How did you handle it? Are you still feeling grief now?

Against Your Heart

Have you ever been forced to do something that went against your deepest sense of who you are? How did that make you feel? How did you deal with it?

Healing Your Heart

When you feel down, how do you help yourself feel better?

Dreams Come True

Do you have a big dream? Write about it and how you will accomplish it.

Helping Others

What is your favorite way to help other people? Why?

Chapter 7
MINDFUL ME at Home

Home can be a safe place where you escape from challenges and find family support. But it can also be a place of conflict.

You live with other people who have needs and demands that may not be the same as yours. You may want quiet so you can do your homework, but your sibling is blasting music. You may want to watch television or play on an electronic device for hours, but your parents set limits. Perhaps you have responsibilities you don't feel like handling.

The truth is, life is always demanding, and the rules keep changing, even at home. You have to find balance, especially in situations you cannot control. This is where mindfulness helps. It won't take away those challenges or "fix" the outside world, but it can help you find inner strength and flexibility.

MINDFUL ME Senses

An easy way to practice mindfulness at home is to pay attention to your five senses:

Seeing

Hearing

Smelling

Tasting

Touching

When you focus on one of your senses, you bring your awareness to the present moment. The NOW. You stop thinking of what happened in the past or what's going to happen in the future. You become more aware of how you are interconnected with your surroundings at this very moment.

At any time, take a MINDFUL ME MOMENT, and focus on one sense. You could choose hearing, seeing, tasting, or smelling, for example. What do you hear when you wake up? What do you see out your window?

What do you taste for breakfast? What do you smell? Put all of your attention on one sense.

Choose one sense for the focus of the day. You can remind yourself by saying something like, "Today I will notice what I smell every time I walk in or out of a room."

Here are some suggestions for practicing MINDFUL ME senses.

MINDFUL ME Seeing

Sometimes we miss out by not paying attention to where we are. Strengthen your powers of seeing by noticing one new thing every day for a week. Perhaps a flower has blossomed. Or your teacher has a new haircut. Or a new poster is hanging on a wall you always pass. You could use the MINDFUL ME Activity Book to keep track of what you notice.

MINDFUL ME Hearing

Stop wherever you are, and close your eyes. Listen to the sounds around you. Is one sound louder than another? Can you hear faraway sounds? What about sounds close by? Focus all of your attention on sounds.

Another way to try this exercise is to close your eyes and ask someone to ring a bell. Listen to the bell sound until you cannot hear it anymore. What sounds do you hear after the bell ringing is gone?

MINDFUL ME Smelling

You can try a smelling exercise with another person. Close your eyes, and ask someone to put an object into your hands. Try this with something that has a strong scent—a flower, an herb, or a piece of fruit. (Do not use chemicals, perfumes, or soiled objects. And be sure not to pick something that can cause an allergic reaction.) Keep your eyes closed, and describe the smell to your friend.

Is the scent sweet or sour? Sharp or mild? Notice what happens in your nose when you smell. Does it tickle? Do your eyes water? What other physical sensations do you notice when you smell?

MINDFUL ME Tasting

Do you gulp down your food when you eat? Do you watch TV or play electronic games during meals? Do you even notice your food?

Mindless eating can hurt your body. You could end up with a stomachache from eating too much. Or you might be cranky and tired later from not eating enough. Try MINDFUL ME tasting instead.

Look at the food on your plate before you pick up a spoon or fork. Notice the food's shape and color. Close your eyes and smell it.

Now take one mouthful. Notice your food on your tongue for a second, and then chew slowly. What do you taste first? Is it salty, sweet, or bitter? Is the texture crunchy or chewy? Where in your mouth do you taste the flavors?

Make your bite last as long as possible. Chew it to a paste before you swallow. Then take three MINDFUL ME BREATHS before you eat a second bite.

What did you notice by MINDFUL ME tasting? Was it strange to eat so slowly? Try it with your friends or family. Could you eat an entire meal slowly and mindfully like that?

MINDFUL ME Touching

You touch things all day—sheets, clothes, doorknobs, faucets, spoons, books, and so forth. The list goes on and on. Keep a record of all the items you touch in one hour. Notice the texture of each object. Is it soft, smooth, rough, hard, abrasive, sharp?

You can record the details of what you notice in your MINDFUL ME Activity Book, or in your binder.

MINDFUL ME Moving

Have you ever entered a room and forgotten what you wanted? Have you ever bumped into someone or something by accident? Most of us have done that at least once.

Try MINDFUL ME moving to increase your awareness of this everyday activity.

Find a room that has a clear path in front of you. Start on one side of the room, and move in a straight line to the other side. Walk ten steps without talking. Concentrate on your feet.

Or, if you move with special equipment, pay attention to all the little details of how it operates as you go forward.

If you are walking, lift one foot slowly and feel every muscle in your leg. Plant your foot, and feel the pressure in your foot muscles as it comes down. Finish one step before you lean forward and lift your other leg.

Move as slowly as possible. If you start thinking about something, stop and pay attention to your feet or your equipment again. When you turn, notice the small movements you make.

How does it feel to put all your attention on moving? How is it to move with nowhere special to go?

Catching Distraction

Distraction is something everybody knows about, right? Imagine this scene: You are in the school library doing a special project. You have to research your topic—the phases of the moon, for example—on the computer. You are finding information about the new moon and the gibbous moon, and you're taking notes. But then you notice something on the internet about your favorite band. You start dreaming about going to their concert and meeting them before the show. Suddenly, your teacher walks behinds you and clears her throat. You look up and realize library time is

up—and you're only halfway done with your research. Oops! Now what?

One way to improve your attention is to notice whenever you are distracted—in any situation, from brushing your teeth to listening in class. When you catch distraction, **you are being** MINDFUL! Just notice how you were distracted, and bring your attention back to the present moment and to whatever you were doing. If you do this during meditation, you will become really skilled at bringing your attention back. But you can do it all day long too. Here are some ideas. Let them help you come up with ideas of your own.

Catching Distraction

- Notice when you eat without tasting your food.
- Notice when you bump into someone when you move.
- Notice when you are not listening in class.
- Notice when someone calls you, and you don't hear.
- Notice when you read without full attention.
- Notice when you interrupt when someone is talking.
- Notice when you are thinking of what you want to say when someone else is talking.
- Notice when you don't hear what someone tells you.
- Notice when you look at social media when you're doing your homework.

MINDFUL ME Homework

Homework! Sometimes it's the last thing you want to do. But the assignment is due, and you need to focus.

When your brain feels stuck from thinking too much, try a brain break, then sit for a short meditation, then return to your homework.

Brain Breaks

Snap and Wink: Wink your left eye while you snap your fingers on your right hand. Switch sides, and wink your right eye and snap your left fingers. Switch back and forth as fast as you can twenty times. (You'll look silly but it's fun.)

Crisscross: Stand up, raise your arms, and wave them crisscross in front of you twenty times. Next, march in place, and touch your right elbow to your left knee. Then touch your left elbow to your right knee. Switch left and right, marching twenty steps in place.

Figure Eights: Stand straight, and make ten figure eights in the air with your right arm. Then make ten figure eights with your left arm. Finally, make ten figure eights with both arms, crossing your arms in front of you.

Sit, Hold, and Breathe: Sit in a MINDFUL ME POSTURE, and lift both arms over your head, palms facing each other. Close your eyes, and take three MINDFUL ME BREATHS. Exhale into the space between your arms.

Imagine you have the entire universe between your arms. Feel the space around you. Imagine you are nothing but empty space.

When your arms are tired, drop them and place your hands on your thighs or in your lap. Settle into your seat. Pay attention to the physical sensations in your body. Feel your breath coming into your lungs and belly, and going out again.

Rest in meditation for as long as you feel comfortable. If you start thinking about what you need to do, take three more MINDFUL ME BREATHS.

Before you finish, set a positive intention to stay mindful for the rest of your day.

MINDFUL ME Media

Most of us rely on electronic devices every day. Teachers want you to use them to stay organized and do homework. You need them for research. You use apps to listen to music, take photos, make videos, play games, contact friends, and check in with social media.

But, too much of a good thing could be hurtful if you are not mindful of how you use your electronic devices and social media.

What do you do when you get a message you don't want to answer? Maybe you think about it even when you want to forget it. Or perhaps you answer too quickly without choosing your words carefully.

Send it? Don't send it? Have you ever been there?

Devices connect you to people, but they can also separate you. Have you ever tried to talk to someone who wasn't listening because they were looking at a phone or playing a video game? Or, have you ever felt angry and agitated when someone asked you to put away a device? Do you feel as if you're missing out if you're not always checking social media?

Ask yourself what would happen if you took a social media break. Try it some time. Turn off your devices for a full day. Notice how that makes you feel.

Hurtful Messages

Let's talk about cyberbullying. Have you been the victim of hurtful messages on social media? How did that make you feel? What did you do about it? Sometimes you cannot stop it, and you need to find a way to keep your own sense of balance and not fight back and make the situation worse. The best approach may be:

- not to respond
- to block the cyberbully on social media and on your phone
- not to blame yourself
- to show hurtful messages to an adult and ask for help.

Report cyberbullying at school. Tell a counselor, teacher, or coach. Keep the message as evidence of what you received by taking a screenshot of the post. Then take a MINDFUL ME approach as you would in any conflict. You may not be able to change the cyberbully's behavior, but you can be in control of your own.

Have you ever read a hurtful message about someone else? Have *you* been tempted to share it with others? It's easy to believe a negative message without asking if it is true or if it might hurt someone. Don't bite the cyberbully hook and spread hurtful messages. Do the opposite. Be part of the solution against cyberbullying.

How Do You Stay Mindful with Electronic Devices?

First, set a limit and stick with it. If that's hard to do, ask someone to help you. Choose times to turn off all devices—at meals, during homework time, an hour or two before bed, and during the night. You can set your devices to Do Not Disturb at specific times. You might be surprised how free you feel when you give yourself a media break.

Second, train yourself never to say anything on social media that you would not say in person. Before you send any message, think about how you would feel receiving it.

Third, if you think you are missing out by turning off a device, remind yourself of what you are gaining by paying full attention to your friends, family, and activities.

MINDFUL ME Bedtime

Sleep is good for you. It's like a reset button for your brain and body. Shoot for nine to eleven hours of sleep a night to be in top shape. Being mindful at bedtime helps you have a good night's sleep.

So, how do you do that?

• During the day, talk out your concerns with an adult you trust. Try not to bring worries with you to your pillow.

• Choose to exercise during the day. This helps you sleep more deeply.

• Eat healthful meals. Avoid caffeinated drinks, chocolate, and other sugary foods close to bedtime. They often make sleep more difficult.

• Put troublesome thoughts into your **Mind Safe** for the night.

• Avoid disturbing TV or video games before bed.

• The light of computer and phone screens wakes up your brain. Avoid using devices an hour or two before bed.

• Turn off phone alerts and message sounds so they don't wake you up at night.

• If you use your phone as an alarm clock, switch to an ordinary alarm clock instead.

Or, put your smart phone on Do Not Disturb and set an alarm that will still ring.

• Avoid arguments before bed. Let it wait.

• At bedtime, remind yourself of one thing that makes you grateful.

• Practice MINDFUL ME meditation before you sleep.

• If you wake up at night, try taking ten MINDFUL ME BREATHS. Count your breaths as you breathe. The **Cloud Floating** and **Hold and Release** exercises might help you return to sleep.

• Keep a sleep journal, and write down how many hours you sleep. Keep notes on when you have trouble falling asleep or if you wake up during the night. If you sleep well, write that down too. You can also keep a dream journal if your dreams are waking you up. This will help you understand whatever is on your mind at night.

- If these suggestions don't help you sleep well, talk to an adult you trust. Your doctor might have good suggestions too.

Journal Prompts

Catching Distraction

Describe a time when you were distracted. What happened? How did you feel when you noticed you were distracted? How did you bring yourself back to mindfulness?

Brain Breaks

Have you ever had a tough time concentrating on homework? What helped or didn't help you?

Social Media

Describe a time when using social media made you feel upset. Did you make any changes after that experience?

My Way

How do you deal with not having things your way at home? Can you let them go? Why or why not?

MINDFUL ME PRACTICE

What is the best thing about doing MINDFUL ME PRACTICE at home? Which activity is your favorite to help you focus?

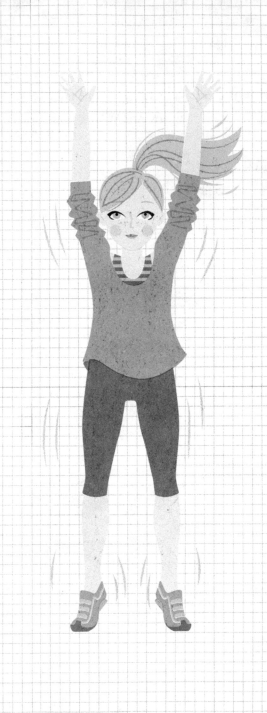

Chapter 8
MINDFUL ME Outside

Take your mindfulness with you when you leave home. An easy way to do that is to choose one mindful quality from the MINDFUL ME mindset chart and stick with it for the day. You can pick from the following list, or think of your own MINDFUL ME quality. It might help to repeat the mindset word to yourself during the day to remember your intention.

MINDFUL ME Mindset

Patient	Curious	Forgiving
Trusting	Kind	Nonjudgmental
Warmhearted	Friendly	Generous
Gentle	Open-minded	Accepting
Honest	Respectful	Helpful
Unselfish	Wise	Grateful

See It through THEIR Eyes

We go through our day seeing the world in one way—
our own way. We think about how things affect us personally. Our mind is trained on *me, me, me*.

But we forget that other people live in different houses, eat different food, have different families and customs, and interpret life and events differently from the way we do.

Let's pretend someone at your school came from another country where people eat only freeze-dried purple food. This new student had never seen anything else and is afraid to eat school food. At lunch, she opens her box of freeze-dried purple food, and all the kids around her laugh at her.

But if you stop and see the situation through the new girl's eyes, you might understand her fear of strange foods. If you were to travel to her country, you might have to eat freeze-dried purple food or go hungry. Or, you might be laughed at if you ate a peanut-butter sandwich or a slice of pizza.

Every day, give yourself the exercise of seeing an event through someone else's eyes. If you don't know what another person is experiencing, ask respectfully and listen mindfully. You never know. You might want to make a new friend, try something new, and learn from an experience you have never had before.

I Hear You

We all want to be heard. Practice MINDFUL ME LISTENING when another person is talking. Focus all your attention on what the other person is saying. If you start thinking about what you want to say next, put that on hold. You will have your chance later. Go back to listening to the other person with an open mind.

When your friend finishes talking, show that you were listening with full attention. You could tell your friend, "I heard you say..."

Take turns talking and listening. Ask your friend to listen to you and tell you what he or she heard.

Kindness On the Spot

You become stronger when you are kind to yourself and others. Try kindness on the spot. Here are some ideas to get started. Add your own to the list.

- Clean your room, or help out another way at home.
- Let someone use something you treasure.
- Rake leaves.
- Water plants.
- Help someone at school or in your community.
- Pick up trash.
- Act friendly to the new person in your class.
- Talk to someone who is shy.
- Listen to someone without interrupting.
- Play games for fun, not to win. Include everyone.
- Shelve books at school or at your local library.
- Volunteer at a club or community center.
- Hold a bake sale, and donate the profits to a cause.
- Give away your old clothes and toys.

Building a Strong Community

Helping others is one way to build a strong community. But sometimes people may not want your help. That's their right.

It's not your job to tell people what they need. You don't know how they might be feeling inside. If you can help someone, do it with kindness. If you can't, walk away, and let it go.

We are each responsible for our own actions. As we have discussed, self-care is also an important part of mindfulness. You can always share what you have learned in MINDFUL ME PRACTICE with others, if they want to know more. Be careful, though, not to force your ideas on other people.

Question Your Own Negative Attitudes

Every day, you deal with many types of people. This is not always easy. Some people like what you like. Some don't. People might call your habits "weird." Or, you might judge what other people do as strange.

Differences do not make us better or worse, only different. If we were all the same, life would be boring. As tough as it might be, we need to respect each other to get along.

If you notice you are thinking or saying negative

things about other people, try looking at them with more kindness. Question your *own* attitudes, and ask yourself why you are critical. What does your judgmental attitude tell you about *yourself*? Maybe you have been taught to believe a certain way about people who are different. Ask yourself if you could open your mind.

Try out new thoughts. Ask new questions.

For example:

If you think:	Ask yourself:
He's ugly.	What does he like to do?
She wears weird clothes.	What are her traditions?
He eats gross food.	What do we have in common?
She keeps to herself.	Could we be friends?
He's acting stupid.	What are his struggles?
She's a loser.	What is her hidden talent?
They're weird.	Am I afraid of the unfamiliar?
I'm weird.	Can I celebrate my individuality?

Problem Solving—In Simple Steps

When you are in a conflict with someone else or a group of people, find a solution. Here are some steps you could take:

1. Calm down before you do anything else.

2. Remember these practices:

   BFF—breathe, focus, and feel.

   Finding the Gap between breaths.

   Holding the Heat, if you are really worked up.

3. Use words to describe the problem to other people. Try not to blame others or yourself. Accept responsibility for your feelings and actions in the situation. Describe the situation with facts, and identify the conflict.

4. Together, think of many solutions. You may have to compromise here. But your needs are important too. Use MINDFUL ME listening when others are talking.

5. Agree on a solution and try it.

6. If you can't agree on a solution, call in a peacemaker—someone who is neutral. Ask that person to choose a solution, and agree to stick with the choice.

MINDFUL ME Friendships

How do you interact with your friends? Answer the questions below to learn more about your friendship style.

1. A new student starts at your school. Do you:
- A. go up and start talking to the new student?
- B. avoid the person and stick with the friends you already have?
- C. bring a group of your friends over to meet the new student?

2. Someone in your class is having a big party, but one student was left out. Do you:
- A. ask the party host to invite the student who was left out?
- B. refuse to go to the party unless everyone's included?
- C. plan something else with the student who was left out?

3. You have a fight with a friend. Do you:
- A. call to apologize and make up?
- B. stay mad and quit being friends?
- C. wait for your friend to apologize first?

Your Friendship Style Is...

If you chose mostly *A* answers, you may like making friends and are brave at accepting your role in a friendship. Just remember that other people may be more shy or hesitant at making friends.

If you chose mostly *B* answers, you may have strong emotions and opinions. You may also feel best with the friends you know well. You could ask yourself if holding on to anger is more important than saving a friendship. Only you know the right answer.

If you chose mostly *C* answers, you probably value friendship deeply and want others to do the same. If you always wait for a friend to apologize first, you might lose something important to you. Make your choice wisely.

Journal Prompts

Letting Go

How do you deal with not having things your way? Can you compromise or let things go? Why or why not?

Renewing Friendship

Have you ever misjudged someone when you first met? What happened? Why did you change your mind later?

Problem Solving

Describe a conflict or problem you helped to resolve.

Your Heart in the World

We are all connected on this planet—humans, animals, plants, and even microbes. Where do you fit in? Write about it.

Mindset

Write about your favorite MINDFUL ME Mindset to practice. What makes it your favorite?

Chapter 9
Moment by Moment,
Ever Changing

If you are reading this chapter, you probably made it through this whole book. Did you try out the meditations and activities? How did that go? Is MINDFUL ME PRACTICE easy or a challenge? Or somewhere in between?

Do you remember that important message at the start of the book? **Mindfulness takes practice.** You may need to work on it as you would any other skill. A soccer player practices footwork. A dancer trains muscles. A mathematician solves problems step by step. You cannot master your mind without practicing MINDFUL ME skills every day.

Before you go away with the idea that this book will make you perfect, let's review the definitions of mindfulness and meditation.

- **Mindfulness means paying attention, on purpose, to what's happening around you and inside you right now, without judging things as good or bad.**
- **Meditation is staying alert and resting your mind in its calm, relaxed, and natural state.**

These definitions say nothing about mindfulness making you good or bad, right or wrong. Those are *labels* and *judgments*—your jigsaw puzzle pieces.

Mindfulness will not make you perfect. But it could make you happier about being yourself.

So, remember, mindfulness is a choice. *Your* choice. Being a MINDFUL ME is about connecting the dots between **feeling** an emotion, **thinking** a thought, and **acting** on them. It is about using meditation to train your mind and expand your heart.

Without mindfulness, you might react quickly to your thoughts and feelings, and do something you'll wish you hadn't. With mindfulness, you can find your way to your WISDOM MIND, which is open, accepting, and generous.

Everything in the world changes from one minute to the next. That's true for your thoughts and feelings too. If you were distracted a minute ago, remember that minute is over. You have another chance to be mindful in this present moment. With each new breath, you can pay attention.

Be mindful **NOW**.

And **NOW**.

And **NOW**.

Do your best in each moment. And thank yourself for being a MINDFUL ME.

MINDFUL ME Glossary

Acceptance: understanding without judgment

Compassion: understanding the feelings of others and
wanting to help

Distraction: an obstacle to attention

Emotion: a strong feeling

Focus: the concentration of mental energy

Meditation: staying alert and resting your mind in its calm, relaxed, and natural state

Mind: the part of a person that thinks, feels, and is aware

Mindfulness: paying attention, on purpose, to what's happening now without judging things as good or bad

Mindful Dedication: offering the benefits of meditation to someone else

Mindful Intention: your reason or inspiration for meditation

Mindset: your mental attitude

Posture: the way you hold your body when sitting or standing.

Present-Moment Awareness: awareness and recognition of what is happening now

Wisdom Mind: inner intuition or knowing

Great Job!

You are now a certified MINDFUL ME. What did you learn about yourself? Was anything surprising? Don't let your self-exploration stop here. As you grow and change, and as life changes around you, you might discover new challenges. Keep on practicing. Your WISDOM MIND will always guide you to your strengths.

Certificate of Completion

in

MINDFUL ME

This certificate is presented to

....

The above-mentioned person is congratulated on taking steps to discover the MINDFUL ME within.

MindfulMe—PeacefulMe LLC
Certified

Whitney Stewart

Whitney Stewart
Author and Mindfulness Instructor

Contact Us

Do you have questions or want to talk about MINDFUL ME PRACTICE?

Write to us at: www.WhitneyStewart.com.

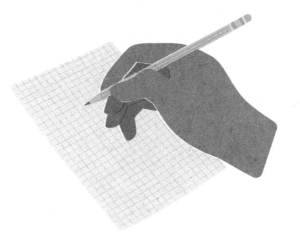

MINDFUL ME

Activity Book

Whitney Stewart

pictures by
Stacy Peterson

978-0-8075-5146-2 • Available Now!

Don't Miss the
Mindful Me Activity Book!

Being mindful won't take away your problems, but it can help you handle them. In this full-color activity book, you will learn to settle your thoughts and look inward through a series of fun writing prompts, games, and meditation exercises. Serving as a guide to reflect upon the lessons learned in *Mindful Me,* it offers you a place to record your reflections, creating a tangible account of how far you've grown in your meditation practice.

MINDFUL ME Intention

Before you meditate, ask yourself why you are meditating. Your answer is your intention. It guides your practice and gives it strength.

Sample Intentions:

I meditate to handle my worries better
I meditate on sharing kindness with other people.
I meditate for peace of mind.

Your Intentions:

I meditate to..

I meditate to..

I meditate to..

8

MINDFUL ME Dedication

Dedicating your meditation is like sealing it with kindness. You offer the benefits you receive from meditation to someone else. You could dedicate it to your best friend, to a special family member, or even to your pet. It's your choice.

This reminds you that you are part of a community of people who all want to be happy, just like you.

Sample Dedications:

I dedicate my meditation to kids like me who feel mad or sad sometimes.
I dedicate my meditation to my best friend who needs help.

Your Dedications:

I dedicate my meditation to..

I dedicate my meditation to..

I dedicate my meditation to..

9

About the Author

 Whitney Stewart travels far for a story. She has trekked in the Himalayas with Sir Edmund Hillary, interviewed the Dalai Lama in India, visited remote Buddhist monasteries in Nepal and Tibet, and sat for days in meditation retreats. When she is not writing or traveling, she teaches mindfulness and meditation to children and young adults.